AN INTRODUCTION TO BIBLE PROPHECY

AN
INTRODUCTION TO
BIBLE PROPHECY

JACK HAY

JOHN RITCHIE LTD
CHRISTIAN PUBLICATIONS

40 Beansburn, Kilmarnock, Scotland

ISBN-13: 978 1 907731 53 2

Copyright © 2012 by John Ritchie Ltd.
40 Beansburn, Kilmarnock, Scotland

www.ritchiechristianmedia.co.uk

Typeset by John Ritchie Ltd., Kilmarnock
Printed by CCB, Glasgow

Contents

Chapter 1
An Overview

The Future. People have always been intrigued with the future, and that fascination has not diminished with the onset of a secular scientific age. In Bible days, the trappings of the occult featured in Nebuchadnezzar's quest for guidance (Ezek 21.21), and soothsaying was alive and well in ancient Philippi (Acts 16.16). The trend lives on, and today, horoscopes, ouija boards, séances and fortune-telling all play a significant part in modern society. The Prophecies of Nostradamus, and Michael Drosnin's The Bible Code have much acceptance with a gullible public. Believers are satisfied that the only safe source of information about the future is the inspired Word of God. Its statements are plain, and it needs no computer to unlock a hidden code. Its predictions have proved themselves reliable, with Old Testament prophecies regarding the first coming of the Lord Jesus being fulfilled in remarkable and detailed ways. That gives us confidence in its predictions of events surrounding His second coming.

A Wake-up Call. Without falling into the trap of interpreting Bible prophecy in light of current happenings, there is a general feeling among believers that events in the world are moving to a climax. Generally, people are dismayed at political conditions across the planet and are concerned about the seemingly endless string of natural disasters. Statements like these are common. "It can't go on like this". "Where's it all leading to?" "Something's got to happen". They have no idea of what that "something" is, but the Bible-believing christian can fill in the blanks and point to the Scriptures with their predictions of divine intervention, a series of events that will culminate in the Lord Jesus reigning in this world for a thousand years.

In one of his books, Dr. Tatford tells of a little girl who was counting the chimes of the clock in the village square. Due to a mechanical problem, the clock struck thirteen times. She ran home and said to her mother, "It has never been so late!" What we call the signs of the times proclaim to all, "It has never been so late". Present conditions ought to be a wake-up call to a slumbering world, but sadly, the last-day sceptics are still saying, "Where is the promise of his coming?" (2 Pet 3.3-4).

World Events. New Testament believers were never taught to look for signs of impending events; they were not looking for signs, but waiting for the Son (1 Thess 1.10). There is no need to dredge through the newspapers every day in quest of significant pointers to His imminent arrival. Having said that, observing developments across the world is compelling, and reinforces the conviction that "the coming of the Lord draweth nigh" (James 5.8). There is an inexorable march towards federalism in Europe which is interesting in the light of Bible prophecy. The re-emergence of Russia as a world force and her sympathies with Iran seem significant, in view of the fact that they will be part of a confederacy that will invade Israel in a future day (Ezek 38-39). The emergence of Far Eastern powers as leading trading nations, allied with their military capabilities seem major factors in setting the stage for events described in the Book of Revelation. As ever, the fluid situation in the Middle East and the constant emergencies that arise leave Israel perpetually in the spotlight, and that is where the final drama of human history will be played out.

Moral Conditions. The moral features of the last days are described in the first few verses of 2 Timothy 3. What is said there is a commentary on present conditions. To be sure, many of the things mentioned have always been a feature of human society, but today, as never before, these things have permeated the whole social order. No attempt is made to conceal what was once unacceptable behaviour; sin that was formerly practised covertly is now glamourised and practised brazenly; "whose glory is in their shame" (Phil 3.19). A few comments on some of the statements of the verses will suffice to show that they describe the present age. "Men shall be...covetous". Covetousness is endemic to society whether it is the benefit cheats at one end of the social scale or the sharp bankers at the other, with their greed bringing the banking system to its knees.

The problem of undisciplined youth is mentioned, an alarming feature of our society. "Unholy": a description of the moral decadence that took root in the 1960s and has blossomed spectacularly in the promiscuity and perversion of the present day. "Without natural affection": hence increased divorce and the abuse of children. The demise of religion in favour of "pleasures" receives mention; religion that remains is declared to be powerless. There is a seeming reference to the tactics of cultists as they worm their way into the homes of unsuspecting contacts.

It could be argued that we are applying these verses to western society, a mere fragment of the overall population of the world. The fact is that with the advance of communications, the standards and lifestyle of western society are being absorbed universally. All over the world, images are being flashed into people's homes, and what is being projected has a baneful effect on their thinking and their morals. 2 Timothy 3 describes conditions universally, and not parochially. For the believer the point is this; if the age of grace is moving to its conclusion with the return of the Lord Jesus, does it inject any sense of urgency into our service for Him? "Occupy till I come" (Lk 19.13).

Object. The goal of this booklet is to provide an introduction to the subject of Bible prophecy. The approach will be elementary, keeping in mind the young believer or the new believer who may be exploring these truths for the first time. For many readers then, it will be merely a refresher course, a restatement of facts they have known for many years, but it is hoped that it will be helpful to "stir up your pure minds by way of remembrance" (2 Pet 3.1).

To say that we are approaching the subject in a simple way may be somewhat misleading, for it has to be admitted that the theme is not uncomplicated. God did not put all the information on the subject on the same page of Scripture. In reality, to get the overall picture we have to draw in details from Genesis to Revelation and look to God to give help to put all the pieces of the jigsaw in the right place. Over the years Bible students have presented different views of prophetic events. The line that will be followed in this publication will be teaching regarding a pre-tribulation rapture of believers with an ultimate 1000-year reign of Christ over the world.

Chronology of the Main Events. There are four major events that must be seen in their proper chronological order, and predictions about other matters fit around these four major events. Later in the booklet, space will be devoted to why we see these events in the order presented here. The first is **The Rapture.** The main teaching regarding it is found in 1 Thessalonians 4.13-18. Opponents of the truth of the rapture state rightly that the word is never found in the Bible. In a secular dictionary the word is defined as follows: "seizing and carrying away", so while the word itself never appears in Scripture, the concept is contained in the words "caught up" (1 Thess 4.17). The word rapture relates not to the Lord coming down, but to the saints being caught up, but His descent will signal their removal. "Maran-atha"; our Lord cometh (1 Cor 16.22).

Subsequent to the rapture there will be **The Great Tribulation**, a phrase we lift from Matthew 24.21. Over a period of years the world will experience unparalleled hardship which if allowed to continue would mean the extermination of the race. Much of the Book of Revelation is taken up with describing the horrors of the tribulation period.

At the end of the tribulation there will be the third major event, **The Appearing in Glory.** We use this phrase to describe the return of the Lord Jesus right to the earth. At the rapture, He will descend only to the air, but at His Revelation, or appearing in glory, He will come right to the earth and vanquish the massed armies of the world as described in Revelation 19.11-21.

The fourth significant future event is **The Millennium**, so called because the rule of Christ in the world will span a thousand years, a phrase that is used six times in Revelation 20.1-10. Subsequent to His manifestation, (another word that Scripture uses to describe His appearing in glory), He will establish His kingdom in this world and rule for that period of time.

Chapter 2
The Rapture

The previous chapter explained the strict meaning of the word "rapture", that is, a seizing and carrying away. That concept is enshrined in the words "caught up" in 1 Thessalonians 4.17. However, we are inclined to call the whole occasion of the Lord's coming to the air and the coinciding events, The Rapture.

The Rapture was **promised** by the Lord Jesus on the eve of His sufferings; "I will come again, and receive you unto myself" (Jn 14.3). The Rapture was **pictured** in the first and last books of the Bible. "And Enoch walked with God: and he was not; for God took him" (Gen 5.24). "A door was opened in heaven...Come up hither" (Rev 4.1-2), and in an instant John was viewing events around the throne. The Rapture was **predicted** by the Apostle Paul in 1 Thessalonians 4.13-18, the main passage on the theme.

Will The Rapture Precede The Tribulation? Is it conceivable that believers of this church age will experience the horrors of the Great Tribulation or will they be removed before that "great and terrible" day dawns? In Scripture there are various pointers to the fact that members of the body of Christ will be in heaven before the storm of wrath breaks.

1. **Imminence.** First century believers were taught that His coming is imminent, that is, it is at hand, it could happen at

any moment, it will be unannounced, no signs will herald it. Listen in to some of their distinguished teachers. **Paul**; "The night is far spent, the day is at hand" (Rom 13.12). **Peter**; "But the end of all things is at hand" (1 Pet 4.7). **James**; "the coming of the Lord draweth nigh" (James 5.8). **John**; "Little children, it is the last time" (1 Jn 2.18). **Jude**; "looking for the mercy of our Lord Jesus Christ unto eternal life" (Jude 21). **Anonymous**; "For yet a little while, and he that shall come will come, and will not tarry" (Heb 10.37). Add to that list the promise of **the Lord Jesus**, "Surely I come quickly" (Rev 22.20). That final promise of the Bible agrees with the promise He made in the Upper Room, where the verb tenses indicate this, "I go…I come again", as if there was nothing to intervene between His departure and His return (Jn 14.3 RV). While there are constant warnings to believers to expect tribulation from men, nowhere does the New Testament instruct them to expect the dreadful age of divine wrath to intervene before the Rapture.

2. **The Wrath to Come.** Jesus is said to be the One who "delivered us from the wrath to come" (1 Thess 1.10). "God hath not appointed us to wrath" (ch.5.9). In Scripture, the word "wrath" is generally, though not exclusively, connected with divine judgment on the earth rather than eternal punishment, and it is a concept that is clearly linked to Tribulation days. "Vials of the wrath of God" will be poured out "upon the earth" (Rev 16.1). The Great Tribulation is incorporated in a period of time called "The Day of the Lord"; that day will be "a day of wrath" (Zeph 1.15). We are promised that we will be preserved from that era of divine wrath. When it is pending, we will need Someone to save us from it, and so "we wait for *a Saviour*" (Phil 3.20 RV), whose timely intervention will rapture us before the storm breaks.

An alleged letter from Paul had led the Thessalonians to believe that their present woes were an indication that they were in the

Day of the Lord. In 2 Thessalonians 2 Paul addressed that misunderstanding. He urged them to discount any thought of being in the Tribulation, and the basis of his appeal was this: "the coming of our Lord Jesus Christ, and...our gathering together unto him" (v.1). In other words, they could not possibly be in the Day of the Lord, for by the time it dawns, Christ will have come and we will have been snatched from this scene. He provided further markers that proved that they were by no means experiencing Tribulation wrath, including the fact that the man of sin had still to be manifested.

3. **Kept from the Hour.** The Lord Jesus promised the assembly at Philadelphia that He would keep them "from the hour of temptation, which shall come upon all the world", a reference to the Tribulation (Rev 3.10). We extend the promise to every believer, for in the context, the Spirit was speaking to the churches. In Jeremiah 30.7, the Tribulation is described as "the time of Jacob's trouble", Jacob being synonymous with Israel. There, the promise is, "he shall be saved **out of** it". To be saved out of it, Israel will first of all have to be in it, but the terminology of Revelation 3.10 is different: kept **from** the hour. Believers of this age will be preserved from entering the Tribulation altogether. It is significant that after many allusions to the church in the early chapters of Revelation, there is no reference to it in the central section of the book that deals with the Tribulation period. She makes her reappearance in ch.19 as the Lamb's wife, and emerges from heaven with Him. How will the church get to heaven in order to appear from it? By means of the rapture; the whole scenario demands that the Rapture precedes the Great Tribulation. The pictures referred to earlier are in agreement with the doctrine. Enoch was raptured before the flood came. John was in heaven before even the first phase of tribulation wrath.

The truth of the Rapture is a great source of comfort for the believer (1 Thess 4.18). Hope would be destroyed if there was the feeling that we have to face the terrors of the Great Tribulation before meeting our beloved Lord.

What will Take Place at the Rapture? As has been stated, 1 Thessalonians 4.13-18 is basic to the subject and unique in its coverage of certain aspects of the event. There are no references to The Rapture in the Old Testament or in the great prophetic sermon that we call The Olivet Discourse (Mt 24-25). That is why Paul stressed that he spoke "by the word of the Lord" (v.15). His teaching was new, but he had received a direct revelation from the Lord regarding it. Critics of the teaching of a pre-tribulation rapture allege that it is so new that it emerged in the 1800s, and the argument is, if it is as new as that it cannot be true! There is no doubt that for centuries it was obscured in the mists of Romish doctrine, but then, so too was the doctrine of Justification by Faith. There have never been any protests from the evangelical world about the re-emergence of that glorious truth.

The descent of the Lord Jesus will signal **the resurrection of sleeping saints**. At death their bodies went to corruption, but He received their spirits (Acts 7.59); they were "at home with the Lord" (2 Cor 5.8 RV). (The metaphor of "sleep" relates exclusively to the body, and the thought is, that there is always an awakening from sleep; there is no such thing as "soul sleep"). That awakening, that resurrection, will take place at the Rapture. It will be the first event before living saints are "caught up". The manner of that resurrection and the nature of the resurrection body are dealt with in 1 Corinthians 15.35-58.

Following the resurrection of sleeping saints there will be **the rapture of living saints** (1 Thess 4.17); living, and believing on Christ, they shall never die (Jn 11.26). Their bodies will be changed in an atom of time to be made suitable for the new environment to which they will be transported (1 Cor 15.51-52).

Obviously, all believers will be entranced with their first sight of their Saviour, but the concept of reunion is embedded in the verses, for we shall be "caught up together *with them*". The thought of being caught up with resurrected believers whom we loved, and together meeting the Lord in the air, and being forever with Him, should be a tremendous source of comfort in a sad world (v.18).

Chaos? Inevitably, when the sudden disappearance of millions of people is contemplated, the practicalities are raised. Driverless cars? Pilotless aircraft? Parentless children? Overturned gravestones? The list of questions goes on. Will there be chaos, or will the event pass in an orderly fashion? Scripture is silent, but on balance, the fact that "God is not the author of confusion" and that He encourages things "to be done decently and in order" (1 Cor 14.33,40) would lead us to suppose that in His own sovereign way He will orchestrate the event so as to obviate disorder. However, no matter how hard people may search, like Enoch, raptured believers will not be found, for God will have translated them (Heb 11.5).

Chapter 3
Events in Heaven

The Rapture will trigger all the happenings leading to "a new heaven and a new earth" (Rev 21.1). Broadly speaking, these events are divided in two, those taking place in heaven, and those on earth. The two spheres are not unconnected, for the Revelation shows that decisions made in heaven, and instructions given there, will impact on events on earth. However, there are three major events in heaven that we must consider.

1. The Opening of "the Book". The "things which shall be hereafter" (Rev 1.19); it is an apt description of the section of Revelation that begins at chapter 4. Before the horrors of the Tribulation commence in chapter 6, space is devoted to an amazing scene in heaven. The throne of God is the focal point, and there comes a stage in proceedings where God, sitting on His throne, extends a scroll on the palm of His hand, a scroll embossed with seven seals (ch.5.1). The challenge rings out, "Who is worthy to open the book, and to loose the seals thereof"? (v.2).

Can we identify this seven-sealed book? Those who are familiar with early customs tell us that its description is consistent with the style of ancient title deeds and Scripture itself gives us that clue. When Jeremiah was buying a field, great care was taken with the legalities of the transaction (Jer 32.6-15). A document was drawn up and sealed in the presence of witnesses, a document described as "the deed of the purchase" (vv.11,12,14 RV). Jeremiah had a certificate proving legal title to that field. So then, if we identify the book on God's hand as title deeds, it begs the question, title deeds to what? As the narrative proceeds it becomes evident that these are the title deeds to the earth, and as each seal is broken, a fresh phase of events is introduced to prepare the earth for Christ to claim it, "The kingdoms of this world (becoming) the kingdoms of our Lord, and of his Christ" (Rev 11.15).

After the initial opportunity to take the book, there was inactivity and silence, a silence that was broken only by the sobs of the Apostle John (v.4). Would evil triumph forever? Would paradise never be regained? Would the devil have eternal dominion? Was there no one to remedy this situation? And so John wept. Step forward the Lamb! Someone is worthy to take the book and open its seals, and as He grasps the scroll, heaven's myriads burst into adoring worship, "Thou art worthy". He had paid the purchase price (v.9 RV), having bought the field for the sake of the treasure that was in it (Mt 13.44). He was the One who had "prevailed" (v.5). Creatorially, morally and redemptively He had established His claim to the earth, and so as Revelation proceeds, He breaks the seals, initiating proceedings that lead to Him taking His possessions. "Ask of me, and I shall give thee the heathen for thine inheritance, And the uttermost parts of the earth for thy possession" (Ps 2.8).

2. The Judgment Seat of Christ. A second major event in heaven will be the Judgment Seat of Christ. There are a number of future judgments that we dare not confuse. Gentile survivors of the Great Tribulation will be judged on earth when the Lord sits "upon the throne of his glory". They will be divided as an eastern shepherd separates sheep from goats. The "sheep" will enter the millennial kingdom; the "goats" will experience "everlasting punishment". The information about that judgment is in Matthew 25.31-46 and we label it, The Judgment of the Nations.

Distinct from that is the Great White Throne judgment, details of which are in Revelation 20.11-15. The subjects of that judgment will be the unrepentant of all ages who have died. They will experience "the resurrection of damnation" (Jn 5.29), their final destiny, "the lake of fire".

Different again is The Judgment Seat of Christ, mention of which is made in two passages of Scripture (2 Cor 5.10; Rom 14.10) with allusions in other places. The common factor to these three judgments is that the Lord Jesus will be the judge (Jn 5.22). For the first two mentioned He will sit on thrones, but a judgment seat is not a throne. It was a raised dais such as was used by judges at the ancient games as they surveyed the events, or what we would now call "the bench", from which a judge like Pontius Pilate passed sentence (Jn 19.13). The Greek word is *bema*, only mentioned so that when preachers use the word without explanation you know what they mean!

Who will be involved? Only believers will be the subject of this judgment. "**We** must all appear before the judgment seat of Christ" (2 Cor 5.10). The "we" in the context refers to believers exclusively, people who have "the earnest of the Spirit" (v.5), people who "walk by faith" (v.7), people who will be "with the Lord" (v.8). *Every* believer will be there, as indicated by the word "all". "*Every one of us* shall give account of himself to God" (Rom 14.12). The reference to the Judgment Seat in Romans 14 is to emphasise that we are accountable for ourselves alone. It is important to keep *ourselves* right, without being preoccupied with the activities of others.

When will it take place? It will be immediately subsequent to

The Rapture. "Judge nothing before the time, *until the Lord come*" (1 Cor 4.5). In that passage, Paul indicates that it is premature to assess a believer's service here and now. The time for that appraisal will be when the Lord comes, so chronologically, we place the Judgment Seat of Christ after The Rapture. "Behold, I come quickly; *and my reward is with me*" (Rev 22.12).

Where will it take place? If it is subsequent to The Rapture it will be in heaven, for that event will see us gathered to Him, to "ever be with the Lord" (1 Thess 4.17).

What is its purpose? Clearly, there is no thought of punishment connected with this judgment; it is judgment in the sense of assessment. The believer's sins were dealt with at Calvary and we rejoice in that glorious fact. "There is therefore now no condemnation to them which are in Christ Jesus" (Rom 8.1). Thus sin is not in question; it has to do with the evaluation of service and granting an appropriate reward; "then shall every man have praise of God" (1 Cor 4.5).

A key thought in connection with this judgment is that we "will be **made manifest**" (2 Cor 5.10 RV). Not only will our labours be assessed but the very motives from which our activity stems; the Lord "will **make manifest** the counsels of the hearts" (1 Cor 4.5). Also, the service itself "shall be **made manifest**...of what sort it is" (1 Cor 3.13). There is a solemn side to all of this. It should impact on our commitment to the work of the assembly (1 Cor 3.10-15). It should encourage us to ensure that our motives are pure (1 Cor 4.1-5). It should deter us from either judging or despising our fellow-believers; we are responsible for ourselves (Rom 14.10-13).

3. The Marriage of the Lamb. Another wonderful event in heaven will be the marriage of the Lamb (Rev 19.7-9), the official uniting of Christ and His church. It is interesting that the occasion is described, not as the marriage of Jesus, or of Christ, or of the Lord, but the marriage of *the Lamb*. The reference to the Lamb is a reminder of the cost to make her His own. It took the sacrifice of Calvary to make all this possible.

Reference is made to "his wife" (v.7). We have help to identify her in Ephesians 5.22-33, where the husband/wife relationship illustrates the relationship between Christ and His church. The wife's subjection to her husband is exemplified by the church's subjection to Christ (v.24), and the husband's care for his wife should be modelled on Christ's love for the church (v.25). Thus the Lamb's wife is the church, the sum total of every believer in Christ from the Day of Pentecost to The Rapture.

Attention is drawn to her wedding dress, "fine linen, clean and white" (v.8). The verse explains the symbolic significance of that; "the righteous acts of the saints" RV. It is clear that here and now we are weaving that garment by honest behaviour, kindly deeds, and integrity of character.

There will be a celebration of that marriage, described as "the marriage supper of the Lamb" (v.9) and opinion is divided as to its location. Will it be in heaven or on the millennial earth? Wherever it is, the guests will be blessed people, but distinct from the bride. These are believers from outwith the church age, people like John Baptist who described himself as "the friend of the bridegroom" (Jn 3.29). Together, they will celebrate the marriage of the Lamb.

Chapter 4
The Great Tribulation (1)

We have noted formerly that The Rapture will precede the Great Tribulation; believers of this present church age will be removed before the storm of wrath breaks.

Descriptions of the Tribulation. "**The Day of the Lord**" is a term used to describe that age. For men of the world, it will come as unexpectedly as a thief in the night, and as inevitably as the labour pains of an expectant mother (1 Thess 5.2-3). The Day of the Lord will be "a day of wrath, a day of trouble and distress, a day of wasteness and desolation, a day of darkness and gloominess, a day of clouds and thick darkness" (Zeph 1.15). It is "the great and the terrible day of the LORD" (Joel 2.31). It should be noted that the Day of the Lord extends far beyond The Tribulation period. In its latter stages it incorporates the dissolution of the heavens and the earth (2 Pet 3.10).

Another phrase that we use to describe that period is **Daniel's Seventieth Week.** In Daniel 9.24-27 there is the notable prophecy of the seventy weeks, a prophecy relating to Daniel's people Israel, and Daniel's city Jerusalem (v.24). The word "week" is literally heptad, a group of seven, and with hindsight, we understand that these were "weeks" or "sevens" of years rather than of days. The first sixty-nine weeks (483 years) have had their fulfilment, culminating in Messiah being "cut off" with the subsequent destruction of Jerusalem and its temple (v.26). Week seventy awaits fulfilment; nothing in history matches the predictions regarding it.

Some suggest that it is inconsistent interpretation to suggest that sixty-nine weeks have run their course with a major time lag before week seventy. However, this is not unique in Scripture. In Isaiah 9.6-7 there is a prediction of the birth of Christ, but then the prophecy jumps the centuries to anticipate Him reigning "upon the throne of David". Isaiah 61 foresees His healing ministry before taking a huge leap to "the day of vengeance of our God" (vv.1-2). Micah foretells His birth at Bethlehem, and then spans the generations to speak of Him as "ruler in Israel" (ch.5.2). In Zechariah 9, centuries intervene between verses 9 and 10, verse 9 anticipating the triumphal entry, and verse 10 the establishing of His universal reign.

The point is, with the rejection of Messiah, God suspended His dealings with Israel as a nation and imposed a blindness upon them (Rom 11.7). The chapter speaks of "their fall" (v.12 RV). It refers to "the casting away of them" (v.15). It likens them to branches broken off an olive tree (vv.16-24). However, Israel's blindness is "in part" (v.25), in that, some Jews are being saved in this present age (vv.1-5). The blindness is not permanent, but only "until the fulness of the Gentiles be come in" (v.25). Thus with the completion of the church age, God will resume His association with Israel as a nation, and Daniel's seventieth week will then run its course. The nation has been sidelined temporarily, hence the gap between the sixty-ninth and seventieth weeks.

The event that will trigger the commencement of the final seven year period will be the signing of a treaty between "the prince that shall come", the Beast, and "many" in Israel, the Christ-rejecting governing class and its supporters (v.27). It appears that part of the agreement is that the dictator will guarantee freedom of worship, with the Old Testament sacrificial system resurrected in association with a temple that will then be in place. "In the midst of the week", that is, after three and a half years, the Beast will renege on his commitment and "cause the sacrifice and the oblation to cease". All religion will be outlawed and he will demand universal homage (2 Thess 2.4). He will desecrate the temple by entering it and masquerading as God, and then his image will be installed there (Mt 24.15). The breaking of the treaty divides Daniel's seventieth week into two periods of three and a half years.

Based on Matthew 24.21 and Revelation 7.14, we are inclined to call the whole period the **Great Tribulation**, but to be strictly accurate that term applies to the second half of "the week". Subsequent to "the abomination of desolation" standing in the holy place (Mt 24.15), "*then* shall be great tribulation" (v.21). A suitable label for the first three and a half years would be "the beginning of sorrows" (v.8). During that time there will be horrendous events on earth, but the full horror of the tribulation will be experienced during the second half of "the week", warranting the title, the Great Tribulation.

The Uniqueness of the Tribulation. The Lord explained that the Tribulation years will be unparalleled in the annals of history: "great tribulation, such as was not since the beginning of the world to this time, no, nor ever shall be" (Mt 24.21). Were it allowed to continue unabated it would mean the extermination of life on the planet (v.22). The world has experienced terrible times in the past. History has thrown up a rash of natural calamities. Plagues claiming millions of lives have swept continents. Two world wars have decimated the young life of the nations involved. It all pales, in contrast to the relentless tide of catastrophes that will sweep across the globe in that coming day. The central core of the Revelation is devoted to describing these cataclysmic events.

The Source of the Tribulation. God Himself will be the major source of the judgments that the earth will experience. It is "the great and the terrible day **of the LORD**" (Joel 2.31). He personally will initiate various phases of judgment commencing with the Lord Jesus breaking the seals of the book (Rev 6). In the presence of God seven trumpets will be given to seven angels (ch.8.2), and as each angel sounds, another horrific deluge of wrath will be unleashed upon the planet. As of ch.16.1, the trumpet judgments give way to the vial judgments, and the angels are instructed, "Go your ways, and pour out the **vials of the wrath of God** upon the earth". Divine wrath will engulf the world and its inhabitants.

To add to the world's misery, the devil will vent his fury against the earth's population (Rev 12.12). Defeat in a conflict in the spirit realm will result in Satan's movements being confined to the earth. It is clear that this will take place at the mid point of the seventieth week for in the chapter there is mention of 1260 days (three and a half years), and "a time (one year), and times (two years), and half a time (six months)" totalling three and a half years in all. Satan's "short time" will run concurrently with the Great Tribulation period with grave consequences for the world at large. In particular, his malice will be directed towards the nation of Israel. Thwarted in his purpose to exterminate her, he will target particularly "the remnant of her seed" (v.17), those who have embraced the Messiah and obey God's commandments.

Some may wonder, how is it that God will have a people on earth during that period? If every believer in Christ will be removed at The Rapture, how can we account for the presence of a people of God on earth after that event? It has already been noted, that Israel is presently blinded, but that blindness is not permanent. When God lifts the blindness after The Rapture, there will be those who will admit the blunder that the nation made in rejecting its Messiah, and they will acknowledge Him. They are described as "the servants of our God" (Rev 7.3). Presumably, they are the servants who will then preach the gospel of the kingdom "in all the world for a witness unto all nations" (Mt 24.14). Multitudes will believe it and for many it will mean martyrdom. Those who survive till the end of The Tribulation are "the sheep" of Matthew 25.31-46 who will enter the kingdom. They are called "the righteous" (vv.37,46). It is a general principle of Scripture that people are accounted righteous *by faith alone*, and thus their kindness to Christ's brethren (v.40) is evidence of their faith; theirs is no works-based salvation.

The Victims of the Tribulation. The main sufferers of the period will be the people of Israel. Primarily, it is "the time of Jacob's trouble" (Jer 30.7). The Lord Jesus said, "there shall be great distress in the land, and wrath upon **this people**" (Lk 21.23). But if Israel will be the epicentre of the tribulation, the shock waves will be felt universally, for it is "the hour of temptation, which shall come upon **all the world**" (Rev 3.10). Even a cursory reading of Revelation shows that the plagues and catastrophes of the Tribulation period will not be localised but will affect the whole planet resulting in a savage reduction in its population.

Chapter 5
The Great Tribulation (2)

Consideration has been given to the duration of the The Tribulation and a number of the catastrophes of that unique period. This chapter will focus on the major players in these horrific years of human history leading up to the benign universal reign of the Lord Jesus.

Israel. Last Days prophecies demand the existence of the State of Israel. For example, in His Olivet Discourse the Lord Jesus spoke of "the holy place", that is, the temple at Jerusalem (Mt 24.15). He referred to "Judaea" (v.16), and "the sabbath day" (v.20), all indications that the Jewish people will be in their land practising their religion.

With the destruction of Jerusalem in A.D.70, the Jews were scattered across the globe, but amazingly, throughout the centuries they retained their distinctive racial identity. Towards the end of the 19th century, the Zionist Movement gathered pace with its demands for a Jewish homeland in Palestine. On 2nd November 1917, in what became known as the Balfour Declaration, British Foreign Secretary Arthur James Balfour stated that his Government would do everything possible to facilitate that goal. At the end of the First World War Palestine became a British Protectorate, and when the mandate ended on 14th May 1948, the Star of David replaced the Union Jack and the State of Israel was born. That very day she was invaded by her Arab neighbours but survived, and in the Six-Day War of

June 1967 took control of Jerusalem and other territories. Israel's occupation of these areas is still a festering sore in Middle East politics. After centuries of dispersion then, now Israel was in her land again. Her final regathering as predicted in Scripture awaits the Advent of the Messiah, but it is of major significance that the State of Israel exists, a necessary prerequisite for the outworking of Bible prophecy.

Middle–Eastern States. Daniel 11 is a remarkable passage of Scripture in which most of the predictions are now history. The accuracy of this history, written beforehand, has provoked the detractors of Scripture to question the dating of Daniel's prophecy and to allege that it must have been written after the events! The believer sees it as an outstanding evidence of divine inspiration. There are two main protagonists in the drama, the king of the south and the king of the north. Malcolm C. Davies identifies these as the Ptolemies of Egypt and the Seleucids of Syria/Palestine, that is, states to the south and north of Israel respectively (Anticipating The End Times p.114). There comes a point in the chapter where there is a leap from what is now past to "the time of the end" (v.40), clearly a reference to events in the second half of Daniel's Seventieth Week. The king of the north and the king of the south still feature, but then they will be allies rather than opponents. Their common foe will be one whose description tallies with that of the man of sin of 2 Thessalonians 2. These latter verses of Daniel 11 seem to be describing the military campaign that will culminate in Armageddon by which time the armies of the Beast will have swept through many lands and be encamped in "the glorious land"; the middle-eastern powers will show resistance to his expansionist ambitions. Lands to the east of the River Jordan will escape his attention (v.41), but that whole Middle East area will be a cauldron, a theatre of war that will be the scene of hostilities of World War proportions, with Israel's neighbours to the north and south being sucked in to the conflict.

Russia. Ezekiel 38-39 predicts an invasion of Israel that appears to be separate from the Armageddon campaign, possibly taking place during the first half of Daniel's Seventieth Week. This conclusion is arrived at by virtue of descriptions of Israel's lack of vigilance at that time. The aggressor describes her as "the land of unwalled villages...them that are at rest, that dwell safely, all of them dwelling without walls, and having neither bars nor gates" (ch.38.11). Israel's guard will be down; high levels of security will be deemed unnecessary; she will be lulled into complacency. It may be conjecture, but it is likely that the seven-year treaty agreed with the beast (Dan 9.27) will involve the promise of military protection, giving rise to Israel cutting the defence budget. The present perpetual state of high alert will be a thing of the past, and so she will be perceived as a soft target.

The early verses of Ezekiel 38 identify those who will be confederate in the invasion, primarily Gog, judged by many to be an ancient name for what is now the Russian peoples. Her first ally is said to be Persia, modern Iran. It is of interest that while Russia appeared to be a very lame duck after the break up of the Soviet Union, she has reasserted herself and has flexed her military muscles. Without falling into the trap of interpreting Bible prophecy in light of current events, it seems significant that Russia remains sympathetic to Iran while most of the world is outraged at her nuclear ambitions.

The object of the invasion will be to plunder Israel, to strip her of her major economic assets (vv.12-13). These plans and indeed the whole invasion strategy will be thwarted by intervention from heaven. A dreadful massacre will take place on the mountains of Israel without the defenders firing a shot. By a divine initiative, in-fighting, epidemic and apocalyptic storms will annihilate the Russian confederacy (ch.38.21-ch.39.8). Such will be the carnage that carrion birds and beasts will gorge themselves on the corpses and it will take seven months to bury the remains (ch.39.11-16). The debris of war will provide firewood for seven years (vv.9-10).

The Far Eastern Powers. Some time after the abortive invasion from the north, there will be an offensive from the east by an alliance described in Revelation 16.12 as "the kings of the east". Enticed by demonic forces, they will march westwards to be marshalled eventually at Armageddon. The great river Euphrates will be dried up to facilitate their advance. On the only other occasion in which the Euphrates is mentioned in Revelation, the context speaks of an army of 200 million (ch.9.13-21). Some take that to be an army of evil spirits, but if you accept it as literal fighting men and link it with the kings of the east, then the invading army will be of massive proportions. The east is perhaps the only part of the world from which the concentration of humanity could supply such an enormous force. Both China and India boast a population of over a thousand million, and other far-eastern lands are teeming with inhabitants. Right now, the Orient could muster the mammoth army of which Revelation speaks. However, no matter how you interpret the hordes that are mentioned in ch.9, their existence and activity will result in the demise of one third of the earth's population.

The Ten Kingdom Confederacy. We resist the temptation to speak of the United States of Europe or the revived Roman Empire, but it is clear that the major power bloc of these end times will be a ten kingdom unit headed by the satanically energised man whom we call the beast (Rev 13.1). There is the suggestion of it in Daniel 2 and 7, confirmed by the vision of the beast in Revelation 13.

Initially, this political entity will be dominated by a religious organisation described as "Babylon the Great" (Rev 17.5); the woman will ride the beast (v.3). This organisation has had centuries of experience of political involvement, exercising massive influence over many of the governments of the world. Her hostility to believers has been consistent throughout all generations. However, by Revelation 17 her days are numbered, and there will come a point when the leaders of the ten nations will resent her interference, throw off her shackles, destroy her influence, reject her demands and utterly destroy her. Her religious activity will be outlawed with everything else that comes under the umbrella of "religion" (2 Thess 2.4). These leaders and their people will worship the beast, and imbibe his infatuation with warfare and armaments; power and weaponry will be their god (Dan 11.37-38).

The blanket ban on religion in the middle of Daniel's Seventieth Week will affect Judaism (Dan 9.27), but undoubtedly it will impact on the preaching of the Gospel of the Kingdom. However, the Lord Jesus did promise that the message of salvation would penetrate "all the world" (Mt 24.14), and despite the obvious perils involved in embracing Christ and renouncing the beast, myriads will respond to the preaching, "a great multitude, which no man could number" (Rev 7.9).

Whatever the initial intentions of each of these various military groupings, ultimately they will unite in opposition to the Lord Jesus when He appears in power and great glory (Rev 19.19-21).

Chapter 6
The Appearing in Glory

The Lord's Second Coming will be in two distinct phases. We described the first phase as The Rapture and we call the second stage The Appearing in Glory, or His Revelation. A period of at least seven years will separate the two. At the Rapture He will be unseen by the world; His Revelation will be visible and public. At the Rapture He will descend to the air; at the Revelation He will descend to the earth. At the Rapture He will come *for* His saints as their Lord; at the Revelation He will come *with* His saints as the Son of Man to stamp His authority on the world. The Rapture will be followed by The Judgment Seat of Christ for believers; the Revelation will be followed by the Judgment of the Nations. The Rapture will precede the Tribulation. The Revelation will precede His kingdom. We now consider this second stage of His coming.

When will He come? The question does not presuppose fixing a date, for "of that day and hour knoweth no man" (Mt 24.36). Rather, it is to establish from Scripture precisely where the event fits in God's programme. It will take place as the climax of the Tribulation period. "**After** that tribulation…**then** shall they see the Son of man coming in the clouds with great power and glory" (Mk 13.24-26).

His appearing is the precursor to His reign; "one like the Son of man came with the clouds of heaven…And there was given him dominion, and glory, and a kingdom" (Dan 7.13-14). In a vivid description of His appearing it is said, "and he shall rule them with a rod of iron" (Rev 19.15). So His appearing bridges the tribulation era and His millennial kingdom.

How will He come? We answer in various ways. First, He will come unexpectedly. For the world, His coming will be as dramatic and surprising as the flood in Noah's day or the outpouring of fire and brimstone on unsuspecting Sodom (Lk 17.26-30). Despite the chaos of the Tribulation days, people will be making every effort to maintain normality, coping with working life and keeping up their social activities: then, intervention from heaven. One can imagine them endeavouring to handle the constraints of the Tribulation, and trying to be abreast with reports of the global conflict when an unprecedented event hits the headlines. The news will be as unexpected and unwelcome as a break in from a thief in the night; there will be a sudden, spectacular, supernatural intrusion to shatter the complacency of a benighted world! The despised Nazarene will appear, and claim His inheritance, and the world will tremble. "Peace and safety" had been their slogan (1 Thess 5.3); now the dream explodes.

He will not only appear unexpectedly, but He will come visibly, as obviously as a flash of lightening illuminating the night sky (Mt 24.27). Many charlatans professing to be the Christ will hide themselves in remote areas or be holed up in "safe houses" (vv.24-26), but their clandestine activities will belie their claims. The genuine Messiah will be seen "coming in the clouds with great power and glory" (Mk 13.26). "Behold, he cometh with clouds; and **every eye shall see him**" (Rev 1.7).

"Power and great glory" will be another feature of His appearing (Mt 24.30). It stands in contrast to His first advent when He was laid in a manger: what apparent weakness: what humiliation. But His omnipotence and splendour will be obvious to all when he revisits the scene of His suffering and shame.

Who will accompany Him? Myriads of angels will be in attendance (Mk 8.38), "ten thousands of his holy ones" (Jude 14 RV), His "mighty angels" (2 Thess 1.7). Also in His train will be "the armies which were in heaven" (Rev 19.14), and their attire leads us to believe that these "armies" are identified with the Lamb's wife of the preceding context (v.8). In other words, believers will accompany the Lord Jesus at His manifestation. It is stated unambiguously in Colossians 3.4; "When Christ, who is our life, shall be manifested, then shall ye also with him be manifested" (RV). It is pleasing to learn in Scripture that on that occasion glory will accrue to Him when the fruit of His travail is observed; "he shall come to be glorified in his saints, and to be admired in all them that believe" (2 Thess 1.10).

Where will He come to? In general terms we have spoken of His descent to earth, and undoubtedly the Armageddon campaign will involve His Presence in different places, Edom and Bozrah for example (Is 63.1). However, at His descent He will alight on Mount Olivet. At a time when Jerusalem is beleaguered, "his feet shall stand in that day upon the mount of Olives" (Zech 14.1-4). The place from which He ascended (Acts 1.6-12) will be the spot to which He will return. The topography of the whole area will be altered dramatically by His descent. The mountain will divide to create an immense valley running from east to west. We assume that the valley will be the channel for a new waterway linking the Mediterranean with the Dead Sea (v.8). Its waters will be "healed", and the marine life of the Mediterranean will pass through to the Dead Sea and thrive in what was once a salt-saturated basin, bereft of life (Ezek 47.1-12).

Why will He come? The immediate reason for His appearing will be to "make war" (Rev 19.11). The last chapter noted that the whole area will be a theatre of war, and as has just been observed from Zechariah 14, Jerusalem will be under siege, with the threat of the complete annihilation of Israel. Just at that point He will intervene. Whatever the reason for them being in Israel, the massed armies of the world will close ranks, and influenced by the beast will have the temerity to suppose that they can pit themselves against the white horse Rider from heaven! (Rev 19.19). With His word, illustrated by a "sharp sword" that will go "out of his mouth" (v.15), He will deal with them, their fate almost reminiscent of a nuclear holocaust (Zech 14.12). "The great supper of God" (Rev 19.17 RV) will then be held when the vultures and their ilk will be summoned to gorge themselves on the flesh of the fallen. This will be in reality "the day of vengeance of our God" (Is 61.2).

Two notable characters will survive the carnage, the beast and the false prophet. The lake of fire will open its mouth to receive its first victims, and these two archenemies of Christ will be "cast alive into a lake of fire burning with brimstone" (Rev 19.20).

What will transpire? With the battle over, the "King of glory" will advance on the beleaguered city. The herald will call for the half-moon "heads" of the city gates to be lifted up in honour of this Dignitary. The doors must be swung wide so that the King of glory can enter. He is "The LORD mighty in battle". He is "The LORD of hosts" (Ps 24.7-10). He will then "ascend the hill of the LORD", mount Zion, the ancient seat of the Davidic dynasty, and assume authority (v.3). He will stand in "his holy place", the temple, for this monarch will combine priesthood and kingship; "he shall be a priest upon his throne" (Zech 6.13). A priority will be the regathering of Israel, and angels will be despatched worldwide to effect this (Mt 24.31). North, south, east and west will be commanded, "give up...Keep not back: bring my sons from far" (Is 43.5-6). However, not every Jew will gain access to the land. A sifting process will be in place at the borders, and only the saved of Israel will be admitted while those who have remained rebellious will experience divine judgment (Ezek 20.34-38). The national repentance of Israel is described graphically in Zechariah 12.10-14 when "they shall look upon me whom they have pierced".

Another major event between His appearing and the inauguration of His kingdom will be the judgment of the nations at the valley of Jehoshaphat, the "valley of decision" (Joel 3.12-14). Full treatment is given to the subject in Matthew 25.31-46, referred to in a previous chapter. The judge is "the King", sitting on "the throne of his glory". Arrayed before Him will be two groups, sheep and goats. The sheep are "the "righteous", who will give evidence of their standing by their works. They will enter "the kingdom" and experience "life eternal". The goats are the "cursed" whose lack of works will expose their rejection of Christ. They will experience "everlasting fire", "everlasting punishment". There will be one further event preparatory to Him setting up His kingdom, that is, the resurrection of martyred tribulation saints. "They lived and reigned with Christ a thousand years" (Rev 20.4). The stage is now set for His beneficent reign.

Chapter 7
The Millennium

When the Lord has ended the Tribulation by His appearing, He will establish His kingdom in this world for one thousand years. The phrase "a thousand years" or "the thousand years" is used six times in Revelation 20, and hence we call that period of time The Millennium. Scripture has decreed, "**He must reign**" (1 Cor 15.25).

A Literal Kingdom. Daniel 2 contains a prophecy that spans an era described by the Lord Jesus as "the times of the Gentiles" (Lk 21.24). During that time great Gentile empires dominate the political landscape. That period will "be fulfilled", that is, it will be brought to an end, and this is described pictorially in Daniel 2. "A stone...cut out without hands" smashes the image that depicts these great empires (v.34) and becomes "a great mountain" that fills "the whole earth" (v.35). The image portrays four Gentile kingdoms from Babylon to Rome, but the stone and mountain are explained like this. "The God of heaven (shall) set up a kingdom, which shall never be destroyed" (v.44). If the other empires are literal kingdoms controlling their territory for their divinely allotted span, it is only logical to interpret God's kingdom in the same manner, an administration that will govern the world in a literal and physical way.

Presently the Lord Jesus does exercise control over the lives of His people, and His realm is spiritual in character, a kingdom into which we were introduced at conversion (Col 1.13). But that does not militate against the concept of literal divine government in this world in a day to come. The Scriptures nowhere predict that preaching the gospel will imperceptibly push back the frontiers of evil and effect a gradual acceptance of Christ until He is acknowledged universally. Rather, He will impose His authority dramatically and instantaneously by what we call military power (Rev 19.11-21), and rule "with a rod of iron" (v.15). "The Lord God shall give unto him the throne of his father David: and he shall reign over the house of Jacob for ever", a statement that is hard to interpret in any way but literally (Lk 1.32-33).

Satan Bound. During the Millennium, Satan will be bound and incarcerated in the bottomless pit (Rev 20.1-3). He is described in four ways in v.2, indicative of his cruelty and subtlety, his slanderous character and his incorrigible opposition to God and His people. These have been permanent features in human history, kindled and stoked by the evil one; during the golden era, in his absence, they will be virtually non-existent.

Some believe that the devil is bound presently, and that what the Bible speaks of as a thousand years is a figurative term for an undefined lengthy period of time. They see it as this present age during which the gospel is being preached and souls are being delivered from satanic dominion. A surface objection to that view is, that to suggest that Satan is bound is far from true to life and contrary to the Bible's teaching about his present freedom of movement and his belligerence towards believers (1 Pet 5.8).

Moral Features of the Kingdom. Melchisedec stands as a major type of the Lord Jesus, and his very name is of great significance, "King of Righteousness" (Heb 7.1-2). **Righteousness** will be a key aspect of the administration of the Lord Jesus. "Behold, a king shall reign in righteousness, and princes shall rule in judgment" (Is 32.1). The topsy-turvy standards of the world will be readjusted (v.5). "Righteousness shall be the girdle of his loins, and faithfulness the girdle of his reins" (Is 11.5). There will never be miscarriages of justice (v.3), and discrimination will be unknown. The regime will show no favours to the rich and powerful; the poor and the meek will be treated in an even-handed way. Since the inception of human government, corruption, graft and nepotism have been endemic. Summarising the integrity of *His* rule Scripture says, "A sceptre *of righteousness* is the sceptre of thy kingdom (Heb 1.8).

Another feature of His reign will be **peace**, illustrated once more from Melchisedec, "King of Salem, which is, King of peace" (Heb 7.2). The first act of aggression was as early as Genesis 4.8, and later a trend to glamourise violence emerged (v.23). By chapter 14 there was more general warfare, and ever since, the pages of human history have been stained with blood. That will be brought to an end when He reigns. Scripture predicts, "they shall beat their swords into plowshares, and their spears into pruninghooks: nation shall not lift up sword against nation, neither shall they learn war any more" (Is 2.4; Mic 4.3). The tranquillity that will exist is epitomised by the picture of "every man (sitting) under his vine and under his fig tree; and none shall make them afraid" (Mic 4.4). Micah envisages an idyllic rural scene, but what about city life, presently such a dangerous environment? City streets will hold no fears for the "old men and old women". "Boys and girls" will happily use them as a playground. Society's vulnerable groups, the old and the young, will be absolutely comfortable in busy urban surroundings (Zech 8.4-5).

The peace that will settle over the planet will extend to the animal kingdom. Wolves, leopards, lions and bears will co-exist happily with lambs, kids, calves, fatlings and cows. Even children will be able to control them, and the youngest of infants will have no fear of once poisonous reptiles. No longer will there be the predator and the prey; the carnivores will have become vegetarian (Is 11.6-9; 65.25). This is creation being "delivered from the bondage of corruption" (Rom 8.21); it is "the times of restitution of all things" (Acts 3.21).

Health and Prosperity. Evidently, death and disease will not be completely eradicated during the millennium for "the child shall die an hundred years old" (Is 65.20). However, infant mortality will be nonexistent, and anyone dying at a hundred years old will be regarded as having died young; longevity will be the norm. Disabilities will be unusual, for "the eyes of the blind shall be opened, and the ears of the deaf shall be unstopped. Then shall the lame man leap as an hart, and the tongue of the dumb sing" (Is 35.5-6).

The mention of "the poor" and "the meek of the earth" (Is 11.4) seems to indicate that the familiar strata of society will still be in place during the millennium. However, real hardship will be history because of high agricultural yields. "There shall be an handful of corn in the earth upon the top of the mountains" (Ps 72.16). "The plowman shall overtake the reaper, and the treader of grapes him that soweth seed; and the mountains shall drop sweet wine, and all the hills shall melt" (Amos 9.13). Even the great dust bowls of the world will become fertile with "streams in the desert. And the parched ground becom(ing) a pool" (Is 35.6-7; see also ch.41.18-20). Not only will there be fruitfulness, but fragrance, when "the desert shall rejoice, and blossom as the rose" (Is 35.1).

Since the fall, mankind has had to battle against the effects of the curse in order to produce a harvest, but then the fight will be over, for "Instead of the thorn shall come up the fir tree, and instead of the brier shall come up the myrtle tree" (Is 55.13).

Climate has often robbed men of their crops, be it drought, flood, frost or wind. On occasions blight or locusts have curtailed the yield. In that day "they shall plant vineyards, and eat the fruit of them", "they shall not labour in vain" (Is 65.21-23).

The Last Revolt. Everyone who enters the millennial kingdom will be one of God's people, but subsequently, multitudes will be born, a veritable population explosion. Salvation has never run in the blood (Jn 1.13) and the kingdom period will be no exception. Everyone born then will have to decide personally about the King, and be willing to acknowledge Him. These are the "people that shall be born" of Psalm 22.31, and to them it will be declared, that "he hath done this". In other words, the message of the cross will still be preached during the millennium, and those born during that time will trust or reject the King. In heart, huge numbers will reject Him. Openly but grudgingly they will acknowledge His authority. For them, His righteous administration and His stringent moral standards will be most irksome. When Satan is released from the bottomless pit at the end of the thousand years, he will find these hearts to be fertile soil in which to sow the seeds of rebellion. They will be "devoured" by "fire...out of heaven" (Rev 20.9). The golden age will be over, the last chapter of time written; the devil will be cast into the lake of fire, the stage now set for the final judgment and the dissolution of the heavens and the earth.

Chapter 8
The Great White Throne

Human history will end as it began, with rebellion against God. In Eden, Satan incited Eve to disobey Him (Gen 3.1-6), and at the end of the Millennium, he will foment the last revolt against divine authority (Rev 20.7-10). Whether it is in the paradise of Eden, or in the millennial earth, or in every phase of God's dealings with man in between, the human heart is fixed in its opposition to Him (Rom 8.7). The last insurgency will result in the destruction of the rebels, and their deceiver will be "cast into the lake of fire" (Rev 20.10). The verse states that this is where "the beast and the false prophet are", a clear indication of the reality of *eternal* punishment; they had been consigned to that place of anguish a thousand years previously (Rev 19.20). With a thousand years behind them, eternity will still stretch ahead, for they will be "tormented day and night for ever and ever" (ch.20.10). Such horror defies exposition.

The Destruction of the Material Universe. With mankind's final rebellion quashed and the archenemy suffering the flames of eternal judgment, it remains for the heavens and the earth to be dissolved to make way for "a new heaven and a new earth" (Rev 21.1), a condition that we describe as The Eternal State. The dissolution of the heavens and the earth will coincide with the last great assize, the judgment of the wicked dead. The Lord Jesus will be the judge (Jn 5.22), and Scripture says, "from whose face the earth and the heaven fled away; and there was found no place for them" (Rev 20.11). Peter also aligns the destruction of the heavens and the earth with "the day of judgment and perdition of ungodly men" (2 Pet 3.7).

We have more details in 2 Peter 3.10-13. The passing away of the heavens and the burning up of the earth will conclude the day of the Lord (v.10). That era will commence after the rapture, its initial stages coinciding with the tribulation period (1 Thess 5.1-11). Its last episode will be the destruction of the material universe.

The passing of the old order of things will be a necessary precursor to the introduction of the day of God, the eternal state (2 Pet 3.12). Most translations say something like this; "the day of God, *by reason of which* the heavens being on fire shall be dissolved". In other words, before that eternal day can dawn, it will be necessary to obliterate the old cosmos.

Noise and heat will attend the destruction of the universe. Men claim that it all started with a "big bang" billions of years ago when in fact the only noise that accompanied its birth was the voice of God: "And God said" (Gen 1.3). "He spake, and it was done" (Ps 33.9). However a big bang will signal its end; "the heavens shall pass away with *a great noise*" (2 Pet 3.10).

Twice over Peter uses the phrase, "melt with fervent heat", then, "burned up", then, "dissolved", then, "being on fire". It indicates the awesome release of energy that will take place. During the twentieth century, mankind discovered the effects of the tremendous release of energy that results from splitting the atom. What is it that keeps every atom in the universe stable, with its electrons "orbiting" the nucleus? "By him all things consist (hold together)" (Col 1.17). One day He will loosen His grip; the divine power that holds every atom together will be suspended, and the result will be such a release of energy as to completely destroy the material universe.

Men speak of the indestructibility of matter, that is, while every form of matter can be changed or modified, it can never be destroyed. However, the God who created matter out of nothing (Heb 11.3) will assign it to nothingness once more. The God who laid the foundation of the earth and created the heavenly bodies will preside over their destruction. "They shall perish; but thou remainest; And they all shall wax old as doth a garment; And as a vesture shalt thou fold them up, And they shall be changed" (Heb 1.10-12). When we speak of changing our clothes, we do not mean remodelling them; we remove and discard one set and don another. In the same way, the new heavens and the new earth will substitute for the old; we "look for new heavens and a new earth, wherein dwelleth righteousness" (2 Pet 3.13).

The Throne. Solomon's throne with its ornamentation is described in great detail in Scripture (1 Kings 10.18-20), but only two adjectives describe this throne of judgment; it is great and it is white (Rev. 20.11). The first indicates the supremacy of this assize; there is no higher court; there will be no recourse to appeal. The second points to the purity of the justice that will be administered; there will be no miscarriages of justice in this court.

While the occupant of the throne is not identified He is undoubtedly the Lord Jesus, for "the Father...hath committed all judgment unto the Son" (Jn 5.22). His own words are sobering; "He that rejecteth me, and receiveth not my words, hath one that judgeth him" (Jn 12.48).

The Accused. In previous chapters it was noted that believers will be judged, in the sense of being assessed, at the Judgment Seat of Christ. Returning Israel will be judged at the borders of the land. Gentile survivors of the Tribulation will be judged when the Lord separates the sheep from the goats. The subjects of this judgment will be the impenitent dead of all ages, "the dead small and great" (v.12). In Revelation 20.5, they are described as "the rest of the dead", those who have remained in their graves after saints of every age have been raised throughout the phases of "the first resurrection". Their bodies will be raised from the grave and reunited with their souls from Hades, as "death and Hades" release their captives (v.13 RV). This is "the resurrection of damnation" (Jn 5.29). Those lost at sea will not evade the fateful summons (v.13). "Small and great", the insignificant and the influential, will all be arrayed at the throne. That is why, like Paul, we need to witness "both to small and great" (Acts 26.22). They are all in grave danger of judgment.

The Books. "The books were opened" (Rev 20.12), and the content of these books will form the basis of the judgment that will be meted out, for "the dead were judged out of those things which were written in the books, according to their works". In other words, the books contain the records of the lives of unbelievers, the evidence of their sin and rebellion, the facts that leave them exposed to condemnation.

The opening of "the book of life" will demonstrate that while they had opportunity for pardon and salvation, that offer was spurned. The names of believers are "in the book of life" (Phil 4.3). They can "rejoice, because (their) names are written in heaven" (Lk 10.20). On the day of judgment there will be ranged before the throne a vast host whose names were never inscribed in that celestial register. So, the contents of the books, and the absence of names from the book, will combine to see these wretched beings "cast into the lake of fire" (v.15). "The Lord knoweth how to...reserve the unjust unto the day of judgment to be punished" (2 Pet 2.9). Those guilty of every category of crime will be there, but at the head of the list, "the fearful, and unbelieving" (Rev 21.8). Is it an indication that fear of ridicule and persecution hinders some from believing, to their eternal ruin.

The Contrast. The eternal bliss of the saved is in contrast to the eternal torment of the lost. The sweetness of God's Presence will be enjoyed eternally (Rev 21.3). The sorrows of earth, particularly those occasioned by death, will be over (v.4). Pain is another disagreeable factor in our present experience. It too will become history as "he that sat upon the throne said, Behold, I make all things new" (vv.4-5). Abundant and perpetual refreshment will be enjoyed (v.6), and a plethora of blessings, summarised by the phrase, "He that overcometh shall inherit all things" (v.7). Our crowning privilege will be the joy of being with Him to behold His glory (Jn 17.24). Little wonder Henry Durbanville entitled one of his publications, "The Best Is Yet To Be"!

Conclusion. As explained in the first chapter, this booklet has been intended as only a primer on prophecy for the young believer or the new convert. Large areas have been left untouched, so your questions about the finer details of prophecy are still unanswered! It has been an attempt to present the basic events of the future chronologically and in as simple a way as possible: **The Rapture, The Tribulation, The Appearing in Glory, and The Millennium.**

Introduction to Bible Prophecy

An Introduction to Bible Prophecy